Becoming The Friend In The Business!

Going from sales person to trusted advisor.

Gregory Towne

Tacoma, WA
(253)380-0523
GregTSpeaker@Gmail.com

ISBN: 1530900956
ISBN-13: 978-1530900954

Becoming The Friend In The Business!

Going from sales person to trusted advisor.

Preference

I have heard is said that everyone should write a book. And I have always had it in my heart to write a book. Truth be told I have probably started this process more times then I truly care to admit. I had promised my friends that I would one day write a book. I actually stated very vocally at a conference that as soon as I get home I am going to write my book! I always had the intention of writing a great book. The hard part was taking a very logical mind and having to free it so that it would be able to expressively and creatively put a book together.

My first attempt was at negotiations. The hardest part was I was wanting to start page one and chapter one. I quickly became overwhelmed at the whole process and then buried the project (or the computer died, I forget which happened). That same thing happened with me on this book. I'm not sure when the light went off on the top of my head that if I just worked on chapters and sections and eventually it would all tie in and become a book! To this day I am not sure if that is the norm, or the acceptable way for a book to get created, but hey it worked for me.

I remember when I felt in my heart that I wanted to speak and train on a professional level. I was actually at an Advocare training in Dallas TX. As I stood next to the stage and looked up at the crowd I knew that I wanted to get on that stage.

When I got back from Texas I started researching on what to do to get in front of people. I started looking at my industry of Real Estate and the professional speakers in it (two of which I have had the pleasure of talking to in person). I truly went back and forth on if I wanted to be real estate specific. I knew that it was my background, and in the arena that I would most likely be accepted in. But ultimately I wanted to get in front of a larger crowd.

I found some great mentors in the world of YouTube and subscribed to their channels. When most people would watch the news in the morning I was having business development, or sales and marketing, or motivational speeches going on as I was getting ready for the day. I ordered a few books and started reading on the speaking and training business.

I figured out that I wanted to be in the leadership or the sales and marketing side of the speaking and training world. On the advice of some of my mentors I went to the nearest book store and looked at who was writing and speaking in these fields. My first step was to the leadership aisle. It was there that I saw the names of "John Maxwell" who I truly do have a lot of admiration for. I then went to the sales and marketing aisle and noticed several other names that I recognized. In that moment I think I even became more inspired as I wanted to one day have my name alongside those same books!

I spent a lot of time thinking about which side of the fence I wanted to be on. And I probably wrote down several topics and book ideas on each side of the fence. Ultimately I felt that my background in the sales and marketing would allow me to help more people than if I wrote about leadership.

I do believe that everyone in business or sales should write a book. As in the process of researching for this topic forced me to get a lot of things that I had figured out along the way and did it as second nature, I had to now get it on paper and in a way that made sense. I think I tried to walk away from writing this book only a handful of times, and each time I realized that my passion to help someone build and succeed at their business won out.

For those that were rooting for me I thank you. This project did take longer than expected, and only one technology glitch that made me thought I had lost all my work (thankfully I did not). Ironically in writing this book has spun off ideas of future books and topics. It is my hope that in one day just like John Maxwell I will have my own section in the book store as oppose to a book!

Thank you again for investing in this book and dedicating the time to read it. I hope that you will discover great nuggets of wisdom and take the time to put it into your business!

Greg Towne

Contents

You're My Friend First, My Realtor Second   15

What is Your Why   19

You Are Your Brand   25

Prospecting   29

How to Increase Your Net Worth by Networking   33

Creating Connections   39

The Power is in the Connection   45

The Power of the One on One   51

How to Have a Masters in Referral Marketing   59

Follow Up Follow Up Follow Up   69

Staying Connected After The Sale   75

Staying Connected by Providing Value   81

Now Go Forth and Become
The Friend in the Business   87

You're My Friend First, My Realtor Second

Those words were once said to me by a good friend. It was ironic as I am sure that he had no idea that by telling me that would spark a training module and business for me. When he said those words it was almost like the light went off on top of my head and I had realized what it was like to build a strong and secure business!

I have had the pleasure of working with people in several different fields of work. There are those that are in real estate, insurance, financial services, legal, and even in the medical field that I share the same type of business experience with. That experience is not only do we have to be great practitioners at what we do professionally for our customers or clients, we must also become great marketers and promotors of our product or service. In this book you will discover what it takes to go from the person that does (fill in the blank) to my friend that helps people with (fill in the blank).

I invite you over the next several pages to learn the same material that I have used within my own personal team as a top producing Realtor! I have also provided this same type of training material for those in the real estate, mortgage, insurance, legal, financial advising, and even for dentist and chiropractors! This material can be used by anyone that is in a position that you must not only be great at delving your product or performing your service, you must also be great at marketing and promoting yourself too.

You will discover that this book is written first in how to attract business, then how to give great value and service while you are taking care of your customer or client, and then how to provide great value and how to stay connected with your customer or client. You may be tempted to jump to a particular chapter, I would recommend that if you want to get maximum value from this book that you start at the front and read everything in order. A lot of the training material builds off of what was discussed earlier.

I am truly excited for you and what your personal business is going to grow to! I see so many people that are constantly spending money on the newest and shiniest marketing gadget of the day. These people never realize that they have a great marketing and promoting resource that is their current customers and client list! In reading this book you will discover how to build true relationships with your customers and clients and from that to be able to build your business one relationship at a time!

What is your Why?

Before we are able to start any type of business building or training we must first look at your why. Why do you do what you do? What drives you to go out and do what you do? Most people will first respond with "because of the money". I will agree that money does play into this a little. I am going to challenge you to go a little deeper, and look at what truly inspires you and motivates you to get up every morning, get out of bed, and show up for your prospects, customers, and clients.

If money was absolutely no worry in your life would you do what you currently do? Now when I ask this question I am not asking if you would do what you do and maintain the same type of customers and clients. What I am asking is would you do what you do and either maintain the same customers or clients, or would you become more selective on who you take on as a customer or client?

If money was no object and you had everything that you needed financially, and you would not do what you currently do. Then I would highly recommend on looking at what you would do. I would look into taking what you would want to do and figure out how to make that your vocation. I remember when I got out of the US Army and became a department of defense contractor working with General Dynamics I went back to school and finished out my degree in the computer world. Now keep in mind that I did not go into the computer world because I always wanted to work with monitors and keyboards. I did not stay awake up at night thinking about how computers interfaced and how they shared information with each other. No I went into the computer industry because it was the "hot" market to be in.

Now working in the computer industry I do feel that I was a good to great employee. For the most part all my employee reviews showed that I was a great employee and often set the standard. At least up to the point of when I almost got laid off over corporate politics, but that is a story for a different book. I was never passionate about working with computers, nor was there anything that I could feel that this industry would help drive me towards my passion. I always found it a little bit ironic that I could not wait for the weekends so that I could go SCUBA diving or play in the mountains, or travel. And my coworkers could not wait for the weekend so that they could go and play the latest version of their online virtual reality game.

Because I was not able to apply my passion into my work, nor was I able to create a link to where my work was at least meeting my needs for a passion in my life I started looking for something that would fill that need. As they say I started cheating in my professional world. What I discovered was when I went into Real Estate I was able to work directly with the customer, I was able to train new Real Estate Agents, and I felt that I was contributing and giving value.

This is the reason when I have someone ask me how I can work as hard as I do, or how I can put in as many hours as I do I am almost a little confused at them. The ironic thing is that I work harder now than I did when I was in the corporate arena, but for me what I do normally does not feel like work. Now does that mean that every day is unicorns and roses and rainbows …. No and far from it! Trust me there are days that I do question why I do what I do and on a few occasions I have actually told my friends that "I Quit!"

Ironically I will wake up the next day in bed, look up at the ceilings and basically say "Well, if I don't do this, then what will I do?" At that point I get up and get ready to take on the day! That is what I mean by what drives you to get up and get moving so that you can help your customers or clients. I really want you to sit down and spend some time on the next couple of questions;

Why do I do what I do?

What value am I providing for my customers or clients?

What personal need is being fulfilled in me?

What drives me to get up and do what I do?

What motivates me to do what I do?

If your true motivation is nothing more than to earn a paycheck, a commission check, or a bonus check. I would highly recommend that you start looking at something new to do. When you are in a position that you not only have to be great at providing the product or service for your customer or client, that you must also be a great promoter and marketer of your product and service you will need to know what drives you and motivates you to get up on the morning and fight for your customers and clients!

You are Your Brand

What is your brand? Is it who you work for? Is it
your region? Or is it you? Your brand is ultimately a
representation of what difference you from you
competitors. Most people will associate their brand
with the company. I would challenge you to think
above that and consider yourself your own brand!

What are the values that you bring to your customer
or client? If the only value that you bring is what
your company can do for them, well someone needs
to have a very tough conversation with you. That
conversation is about the fact that if you cannot add
any additional value for someone to work with you,
then you are easily replaceable by both your company
and your customer or client.

You have to think on a scale bigger then what your
company or your customers or clients think of you.
When I hear the term "brand" I think of what makes
this particular person or customer different than the
rest. So what are you going to do that is different
then the rest of the competitors that work in the same
industry as you? What are you going to do that is
different than the same people that work in the same
company as you do? What are you going to do that
will make you stand out above your peers?

As we go through this book I want you to look for
opportunities that you will be able to own who you
are and what you do. I want you to look at areas that
you can improve yourself in how you create an

unbelievable experience for your customers or clients. I want you to start looking at how to build your own personal reputation and brand.

Now I can't tell you in this chapter on how to improve your brand, or what your brand should be. That ultimately lies with you, your personality, and for lack of a better word your personal flair. I will recommend that you take your personality and put it part of your brand. It is in this step that you will ultimately begin to own what will become known as your brand!

Prospecting

All friendships start with prospecting. Go back to your first day at Elementary School. You walked in to a class room that you may or may have not known a single person. What did you do? Did you look for someone that had on the same type of clothes? Did you look for someone that looked familiar? Or did you stand off in the corner and waited for someone to come to you? Prospecting is one of those daily activities that we must do not only as sales leaders, we must also do this as leaders in our companies. There are several types of prospecting opportunities. Along with some areas that are normally not thought of as prospecting opportunities. If you think about it, anytime you get a chance to meet someone or reconnect with someone is a prospecting opportunity. I once saw a regional manager at a chamber networking event with a couple of his account executives. The new account execs assignment – to collect 10 business cards and not to overlap each other. The tough thing about not overlapping each other was that neither one of the two could say who they had collected a card from. This actually taught them what I call networking by drive by and neither one of the two account execs made any true relationships that night. I am glad to say that the regional manager is no longer a regional manager.

When you go to a chamber event, or maybe a leads group, or a mixer, or an industry party at a trade show what is your intention for the event? If it is one that you want to collect as many cards as possible? Or is it one that you want to create a few great relationships? We have all experienced that person at a networking event, the one that comes up gives you his or her two minute sales speech then gives you a card and runs off to the next person. When that happens to you what do you normally do with the card? I know for me those cards normally make it the trash before I leave the room. Now let's think about the person that strikes up a conversation with you and ask you some key questions. Questions that may follow on the lines of:

F Tell me about your **Family**
O What do you do as an **Occupation**
R What are things that you like to do outside of work also knows as **Recreation**
M And then if they are able to meet one of your needs, or solve a problem that you may be experiencing then they can deliver their **Message**.

FORM is an acronym that has been taught at all levels of sales schools and trainings. What it does is it gets you to learn about the prospect. It gets you asking questions about them. It helps you learn about them. Then guess what? If they have a need that you have identified that you can help them with – you are able to deliver your message. And since it is centered on their need – it does not feel like a sales pitch. Let's say that you do not discover a need that you can help them with? Can you introduce them to someone that can solve their need? At that point you become a great resource for them and have started building a relationship of trust.

How To Increase Your Net Worth By Networking

When I say networking event what goes through your mind? Is it a strict and rigid networking group that requires you to have perfect attendance and to always bring a guest or a referral? Is it a chamber event? Maybe a trade show? Or is it possibly a class reunion, sporting event, or an informal get together with friends.

So many people only look at "business" networking events as a chance to help increase the people that they know. A true professional understands that every time they around a group of people this is the ideal time for them to build their personal sphere.

Let's first look at what most people consider to be a networking event. This can be a chamber meeting, a business afterhours or trade show. We have all seen that one person at these types of events. They fly through the event almost running from one person to the next. Never building any type of relationship as they feel that the way to classify this get together as a win is by the number of business cards they collect. Now think for a moment, once they get home or get back to the office what happens to this huge stack of cards that they collected? Do they call on them, probably not as what would they say – remember me I was one that talked with you for under fifteen seconds. Do they email them – possibly but what type of relationship was built out of that tactic. Or does the cards that can represent hundreds of thousands of dollars' worth of business just sit there on their desk and collect dust to eventually be thrown in the trash? In this style of networking I refer to as "Networking by Drive by" No real relationship was created, no reason to follow up, and if there was a follow up normally an accord moment of the two people trying to remember who each other was entails.

Now for a moment imagine what it would be like to network properly. What would it look like for your business if you knew that every time you walked into a networking event that you would judge the success of the event not by how many names, phone numbers, addresses, and emails you collected. You would judge the success of your event by how many relationships you created. You would set your standard of success by how many relationships you had improved on for that time now being well spent. Now when you follow up with someone you have a genuine reason for following up and your prospect is now not only expecting your call, but is now also excited to take your call.

How do you accomplish this task? When I walk into a room or event that has the opportunity for networking (which is just about anywhere). The first thing that I look for is what I commonly refer to as "where are my friendlies at". Do I see someone in the room that I already know? Is there someone in the room that I have seen before? Is there someone in the room that I recognize from a different event? The beauty of finding your friendlies and starting off with your friendlies is that it gives you a chance to warm up. A good friend or networking buddy is going to help introduce you to people. A great way to return the favor is to introduce them to people that they know.

In doing this you will help create what I call "The Networking Show" people at networking events get attracted to the larger groups of people. To a certain effect people are a heard mentality group especially when they are in an environment that they are un-familiar with. Have you ever heard the phrase that there is safety in numbers? Well it applies to business events too. Now as your Networking Show starts to grow and build you will notice that people will start hanging out on the outskirts looking to become part of the group. Once again this plays perfectly into how even as humans we are attracted to being part of the pack. Now when you see someone starting to hang out by the edge of the group, invite them in. You will be amazed at the connection that you will build by being the friendly face that brings someone into the herd.

When is it time to peel off a conversation or group? For me when I am in a small group that I am not able to provide value to, or when I am in a small group that the conversation is that involves only two of the people (that does not include me) or when it is myself and someone that is in the same industry as myself (this person can also be known as "the competition") I know that it is time for me to casually "peel off". This can be done in a number of ways, some of my favorites include "it was great to catch up with you".

Another technique is to casually migrate over into another group. For the most part I want to make sure that I do not become the accord person that is standing there.

Now let's take a look at a networking event that most people do not look at as a networking event. These types of events normally are more social, private, and family oriented. Most people do not even think of them as being networking events and ironically I have meet some of my best clients at these events. These events can range from weddings, house warmings, sporting events, or just about anything else that involves a group of people that did not have the intention of getting together for business. Same rules apply here for getting to know people and build a relationship with them. The best part of this type of event is that there is no rush to do business. So it is easier to spend some time with someone to truly get to know them.

On rare occasions I have been in a room that I only know one or two people. This commonly happens at an office party that I may have been invited to, or possibly a party at a friend's house. In this situation yes you start with your friendly – which in this case is probably the person that invited you to the event. You do not want to camp out with this person. For a few reasons but most important you do not want to develop a reputation as the person that needs to be baby sat. In this situation you will need to break out of your comfort zone and have the ability to walk up to someone, start a conversation, or be able to quickly add to a groups conversation. Once again in a "cold room" look for someone that you have something in common with to chat to. Or at least be able to walk up to someone that is by themselves and introduce yourself to them.

Creating Connections – Powerful Questions to Build Connections

So often when we are at networking events we would love to create a connection, but very few of us have had the training to do so. How often have you heard someone ask the question "What do you do?" I often find myself wondering at what point in time we learned this horrible question. Now keep in mind I spent years asking this same horrible question as I did not have the training that you are about to receive yet.

When someone asks you the question "What do you do?" what is your normal response? Most people will respond with "I'm a Realtor", or "I'm a Mortgage Guy", or they identify themselves with their profession. I understand and get that part of what we do does become part of our identity. I want you to go back in time, when your profession was not part of your identity. If someone had asked "What do you do?" Your response may be something more in line of what you enjoy doing, a response may be "I like to SCUBA dive", or "I love to travel" may be the response that someone will give if they do not identify part of their identity with their profession.

Another downfall of being asked this question is that it really does not give the opportunity to build a connection. I have a friend of mine that hates this question and will answer it with something that relates to his personality instead of his profession. The reason that he has given me is that he feels that when he responds he almost feels that the answer he gives will determine the amount of time that person will give him to build a connection.

I have discovered that when I take control of the conversation I am able to truly build a great connection. Also I have discovered that most people are absolutely ok and thankful with me taking control of the conversation, as most people feel uncomfortable being in a room full of strangers and trying to determine how to strike up a conversation.

One of the first questions I will ask someone is *"Where do you work at?"* Notice the difference in this question as oppose to what do you do? In asking this question it allows me to get into a conversation with them. Now keep in mind sometimes I will have the person that responds back with a geographical location. In that situation I will ask them what company do they work at in Tacoma (or Seattle, or Portland, or wherever they answered at).

From that I will ask them *"what inspired you to go into that?"* If inspired feels to personal or intimate then you can ask *"what lead you into that?"* I have asked this question to hairstylist to highly educated corporate CEO's. This one question will do more at building a connection then just about any other question out there. By listening to the response on this question will give you great insight on the person, their morals, and even what drives them! This question I truly do feel will do more to help you build connections with someone than just about any other question out there.

Now I want to dive a little deeper. One of my next questions will be "*what was it like when you first got started?*" Think back for a moment what it was like your first months, weeks, days, hours, and even moments when you first started doing what you are doing today. I am sure that there was moments of great excitement and great fear, possibly all in the same day! I remember back when I first started in Real Estate full time. I was truly excited as this was the first time that I truly was able to control my schedule and my time, yet I was also truly terrified as I knew that I was no longer in a position where I was getting paid to just show up. To this day I can still look back and think about that day!

Another question that I will ask is "*What do you like about what you do?*" Now we can all come from having a crappy day that we wonder why we do what we do. Most of the time even in that moment we do remember what we like about what we do, and this is why we get up in the morning even if we do not want to and go out and take care of our customers and clients. By asking this question this will allow you to also learn and discover what is important to this person. I do not know anyone out there that gets excited to jump out of bed in the morning and says "Boy I hope I make enough today to pay the bills!" And if they truly feel that way you have to ask is this the customer or client that I want to work with.

After asking these questions I want to bring them back to the present, so I am going to ask a question along the lines of "*How do you do (fill in the blank) today?*" This last question will really depend on what they do for a living. This question will help me see what they do on a regular basis in today's working world. As I can think back at my first day as a full time real estate agent. How I work today is drastically different then when I first started.

Now in the course of all these great questions sooner or later the prospect or person you are building a connection with may all the sudden realize that they have done a lot of talking. They may feel a little embarrassed as they realize that they have been doing all the talking and all the sharing, and they realize that they have not asked you anything about you. Now keep in mind that the person that you have been chatting with and learning about probably has not had this degree of training, and that's ok (share it with them later). So they may ask "Tell me about yourself" or worst yet "What do you do?" Now you are able to share with them about yourself, and what you do for your customers or clients, and most important why you do what you do. You will also be able to share with them in a manner that the message can now be custom tailored to your prospect so that they can truly relate and start to build a connection with you. I want you to understand something, and this is very important. If you use this chance to share something about you that is not authentic, or a flat out lie …. When it comes out you will lose all credibility and connection with this person and potentially others. You can custom tailor you message and still stay authentic with who you are and what you do.

I truly feel that the nugget of information I just shared with you about how to build connections by asking question is one of the biggest values of this book. I find myself using this all the time in professional circles, in social circles, and yes even when I am talking with someone that I find attractive and seeing if there is a connection. I would recommend that you study these questions and start working them into your conversations. I truly do feel that you will be amazed at the connections that you will create by asking these great questions!

The Power is in the Connection

Imagine for a moment that you have moved from doing activities to attract a client or customer, to you now have a client or customers that is considering working with you. Or better yet, they have chosen to work with you! At this point you want to develop a connection with this person as this will help take them from a "prospect" to a "client". Now just because someone has chosen to meet with you do not celebrate just yet, as they may be interviewing several professionals before they decide on who to hire. Even if the prospect is a good friend, you want to approach every meeting with your absolute best foot forward.

There is an old saying – with all things being equal people will want to do business with those that they know, trust and respect. I tend to have a slightly different point of view on this. My view is that even when things are not equal, people will still tend to want to do business with those that they know, trust, and respect. I have always been concern when I have a client that wants to compete only on price. If the only way that you are able to compete is on price. You will discover that you are always at the bottom end of the market and traditionally fighting to keep you clients or customers.

Mirror and Matching

Mirroring and Matching is just as it sounds. It is merely reflecting certain actions, items, or words that your client or customer does. Now there is a little secret that you have to remember about mirroring and matching. That secret is that if your actions are painfully obvious, the attempt to connect with your potential client or customer will be lost. There has to be a degree of congruency with this. Any attempt by you or anyone else that is not authentic will be discovered by the prospect and typically will not end well for yourself.

One of the first items to look at is how is the prospect sitting? How are they walking? Do they have their arms crossed? In order to be successful at connecting with someone you have to have the ability to truly pay attention to their physical stature. What is the speed they are walking at? When you are observing them at the physical level you want to look for ways that you compliment them. If their hands are folded in their lap, then you want to casually and subtlety fold your hands in your lap. How are they breathing? See if you can match where they are at in breathing. Keep in mind that your actions have to be subtle on this. If you are squirming in pain to cross your legs in a manner that you would normally not. The potential client or customer will get a feeling deep inside that they cannot trust you. Think for a moment in time when just did not trust someone, you could not put your finger on it … but there was just something about the person that caused you to not trust them

Another way of connecting is with your speech patterns. If I am talking with someone from the New York, I will speak with a different tempo then that of a conversation with someone from Tennessee. Word patterns will also be different speaking with someone from Arizona to that of Florida. I am also going to listen for key words, or pattern of words. If I am able to work these key words or pattern of words into my presentation I typically will. One thing to keep in mind. If there is a word, or slang, or pattern of words that you traditionally would not use – then do not use it. I tried it in the past once, and it came off very unauthentic and the connection that I had with the prospect was quickly lost. The hard part of this lesson that I learned was that this also affected a personal friendship too.

One final thought on mirroring and matching is that I cannot stress enough on how important it is to be congruent. I will be one of the first to say that anyone in a sales and leadership position has to be flexible to a certain extent and be able to change how they deliver their message. The key element is that you have to be congruent with who you are. If not you will come off as fake obnoxious or pushy. All of those feelings are hard to recover from.

How to Communicate

There was once a time when the only way to follow up, or update, or just about any type of communication was either the phone or the dreaded mail service. Now in today's world we have the ability to communicate and follow up in several ways. It would be nice to communicate with our customers or clients in only one way and have them change to adapt to our needs, unfortunately as the professionals we are – it's normally up to us to adapt our ways to meet our clients or customer's needs.

The best way to find out how someone wants to be communicated with is just to ask them. Some people will prefer voice or text messaging. Others will demand email for every correspondence. While others will only look at their email once or twice a day. Some people may want a particular messenger app. The important thing to remember is how they best want to be communicated with.

There will be a day when you will have to communicate something that is less then pleasant to your client or customer. It is in these instances that I truly believe that you will be able to show that you are a trusted friend and advisor as oppose to that if a sales person. It is my belief that most people when there is bad news, want to learn it from either voice communication (not voice mails) or in person. I have had people that would only want to text that I would send the text "Give me a call as soon as you can". What this does if they are in a meeting does not send them into panic mode but in a subtle way lets them know that we need to chat.

I remember one time that a company that I had off and on sent business to along with recommending for our clients had dropped the ball. I realize (just like most other people) that sometimes balls get dropped, things slip through the cracks, and well people are human. Instead of calling me or my staff to let us know that "the ball got dropped" they sent an email out. Worst yet they did not include all parties on the email. I actually found out about it via the other broker. When I contacted the person at the company that sent out the email her response was "well I sent out an email". At that moment I contacted not only my account representative I also contacted the vice president of sales for this company. I told the vice president that if I had delivered this type of news to my clients via email that I would be fired and I would deserve to be fired. She asked me if they were "fired" from doing any further business with us. Well that has been the last time we have done business with that company.

Conclusion

I cannot stress enough the importance of being congruent in how you connect with people. I see people all the time at networking events that run from one person to the next trying to meet as many people as they can almost having an imaginary competition of who can collect the most business cards. The funny thing is it is the people that spend the time to truly connect with a handful of people that really get the best value out of attending a leads group, networking event, or a chamber meet up. Start putting these items into practice and you will soon discover what it feels like to become known as the "Friend in the Business"

The Power of the One on One

Imagine for a moment what would happen to your business if you spent the next six months making a focused effort to build two relationships a month, or an additional twelve relationships. Look for a moment and see what the date six months from now is. As I sit here and write this we are in November. Six months from now will be May, now no matter what I say, do, or try in six months guess where we will be at? Yes we will be in May. Now I have the opportunity that in May I can have an additional twelve relationships just by connecting with two people a month, or in May I can have no additional relationships by not connecting with a couple of people a month. Keep in mind that nobody has the ability to stop or create more time, fortunately we have the ability of how we are able to leverage that time for us.

The Strategic Partnership

Who else serves your typical customer? If you were in the wedding industry who would be also in contact with your customer, but not in direct competition with you for this customer? Some of those people would include;

A Caterer
A DJ
Wedding Venue
Dress Shop
Tux Shop

Jeweler
Event Planner

And this list could go on as long as the wedding budget would allow. Now think for a moment in your particular industry who would make a great strategic partnership for you. Just like in the above example if someone is going to get married they may start with a jeweler first, or maybe they start with the DJ, or possible even the event planner. The lesson to remember is that they are going to start somewhere. We do not know exactly where, but the more strategic partnerships we have the higher ability we have to referral business back and forth to each other.

What types of companies or industries should you be connecting with to build strategic partnerships. Is there a company or industry that is a little outside the box that most of your competition would not think about. In the example of someone in the wedding industry, how many connect with an attorney that works in developing prenuptial agreements. Take a moment and think about who you should be building strategic partnerships with that will assist you in being able to make recommendations to your customers or clients, along with open up the ability for your to receive referrals from those strategic partners?

Make a list of those industries that you need partnerships with, then next to that list start filling in names of those that you trust would deliver the same quality of service to your customer or client that you would. Now start looking at that list and see where the gaps are at. Who do you need to meet to help fill some of these gaps? What networking groups, or chamber events, or associations do you need to attend, join, or get active in to find these people or strategic referral partners? Most important is when do you plan on not just joining a group, but also attending some of their events to discover and build these relationships.

How many people should you have in each of these categories? That is mostly up to you. It really does depend on your industry, location or field to determine how many partners to have in each category. What skill set, customer service, or level of loyalty to building a referral base business do you want to have from your partners? These are all questions that you should look at ahead of time to help you determine who will be a great fit for you and your customers.

Non-Strategic Partnerships

In my business as a real estate broker I have the normal people on my recommendation list that includes;

Plumbers
Electricians
Home Inspectors
Lenders
Title and Escrow Companies
Pest Control Companies

And several others that you would think of when someone thinks of taking care of a need in the real estate field. What amazes most people is that I also have on my recommendation list;

Auto Service Companies
Chiropractors
Dentist
DJ
Attorney
Financial Planner

I know what you are thinking, if someone is thinking about buying or selling their home they would call a chiropractor! I know that is the first person that you would think of. These people fall into what I call non-strategic partnerships, and they can still be a great source of referrals to your business. These industries or people while they do not work directly in the industry that would traditionally help me find new customers, they do have a network of people that trust and respect their opinion.

Think also for a moment of what this means to your customers or clients when you develop these relationships of great people and companies that involve your industry along with outside your industry? Now you are not only the one that they think of when they need help in something you can directly take care of for them, they think of you when you can help them in a problem that does not include your industry. In doing this you have gone from

being the person that I know that does fill in the blank
to my friend that does fill in the blank!

How to Build Your Partnerships
How many networking events do you attend? If you
do not attend many, should you start attending more?
I see so often when people attend networking events
they have the attitude of how many people can I meet
today. Maybe a better attitude is how many
partnerships can I create.

Take your list of strategic partnerships with you to
your next leads group, networking event, or chamber
meeting. I want you to look for someone in that field
to connect with. Keep in mind that just because you
exchange cards, trade emails, or have coffee with
someone does not mean that you have to do business
with or send business to that person.

Also at these events be on the lookout for non-
strategic partnership people. Normally what I look
for in these groups of people is who also provides
great customer service to their clients or customers.
From my experience is that when someone provides
their customers or clients with great service, they will
provide my customers or clients or friends with great
service.

Ideally when I am at a leads group, networking event,
or chamber function I typically look to create one
appointment with someone just to learn about their
business. Now keep in mind I am not looking to book
an appointment so that I can pitch them, or try to sell

them my product or service. Ideally I want to learn about them as a person, what their company provides for their customers or clients, and what interest and activities they enjoy doing. What the last part does is take us from just a business relationship to hopefully develop a personal friendship.

What would it mean to your business or company if you developed just a few new relationships over the next handful of months? What additional value or services can you bring to your base of customers or clients? What new relationships can your partnerships help create for you in your business? This is one of the best ways to become known as "The Friend in the Business"!

How to have a masters in referral marketing

What is the value of a referral? In the corporate valuations world we often will use a term referred to as "cost of customer acquisition". What this is for every marketing program we track what it cost to run the campaign divided by the customers that purchased. As long as their orders are greater than that figure plus the cost of goods (or services) and either meet or exceed the profit margin that is needed. You have a good marketing plan to run.

Now let's look at when someone referrals you to a coworker, friend, or family member? What was your cost of customer acquisition for this customer? Depending on how you look at what I refer to as your follow through campaign (we will discuss this latter in this book). What was the true cost of this new customer? I am very confident that the cost to acquire a referral will be lower than that to attract a new prospect in from general public marketing. I do want to make sure that I am clear on something. I to this day still market to the general public. Although that marketing is specifically tailored to who in the general public, I still to this day run marketing campaigns to stay connected with my current friends and clients along with a much targeted marketing campaign to the general public.

Also keep in mind that no matter what you do, how great you are, and no matter how perfect your follow through campaign is going to be ... some people will never refer you to their friends, family, or coworkers.

There is and always will be a segment of the population that just does not feel comfortable referring someone to anyone. My recommendation is that you still keep in contact with these customers or clients. You keep them on any follow through marketing campaign just as anyone else. Something to keep in mind is that you will never know when they may become comfortable referring you to a friend, family, or coworker. By keeping connected with them with a great follow through campaign will also show that you care about them further than just a pay check.

Now there is a little secret that will help you discover if someone feels comfortable giving a referral. That secret is during the course of doing business with them, ask them do you happen to know a plumber, or electrician, or accountant, or just about anything. You will want to make sure to ask for a referral that is within a field that is similar to yours or compliments yours. Restaurants are typically bad items to ask for as many people will have no problems telling you about their favorite hole in the wall place to grab a meal. Another great reason for doing this, do you still have some spots on your strategic partnerships that need to be filled? If you are hearing consistently the same name – then this is probably someone you should reach out to and set up a one on one.

Stop Asking to be Referred!

Let that sink in for just a minute … I know you just went back to reread that last statement thinking that it must be a typo. Let me say this again – Stop Asking To Be Referred! There now that you know for sure that it was not a typo we can move on. Think for a moment what is the definition of referred. In our terms it means to be introduced, recommended, or this is my guy or gal.

Now let's think about what the term referred means to the general public? When I ask this to my closest of friends and clients the response that I heard was significantly different. Just like you may be I was expecting to hear recommend, or introduced, or my friend that does. Surprisingly what I heard was when I have to go to my doctor to see the specialist that I need to see.

I learned a powerful lesson on this. That lesson was understanding that even though we speak the same language, that word may have a different meaning. When we ask for a referral we look at that as almost like a gift that we cherish. When the general public hears referral they are thinking of hospitals, doctors, and unpleasant medical procedures. Exact same word, different meaning. We have to change our language, so that we can receive what we are looking for.

So what do we ask for? What language does the general public use when recommend a business or someone? Instead of asking to be referred (which is our language) we need to start asking our friends, family, customers, and clients to introduce us to people. An introduction is the language with meaning that our clients and customers can relate to and understand. It also helps them feel good to help introduce someone to their friends, family, and coworkers that will help solve someone's problem. Next time you want to ask someone to refer you, ask them instead to introduce you to.

The Most Valuable Place to Have Your Name and Number.

What is the best place to have your name and number at? I see people's names and numbers every day. These names and numbers are on the side of buses, looking back at me on shopping carts, in all sorts of print and online marketing media. Depending on what your particular industry is these areas of general public marketing can make sense. Would you consider this to be the best real estate for your contact info to be in?

When it comes to getting introduced to your customers or clients friends, family, and coworkers the most important space that your name and contact information needs to be in, is your customers and clients phones. When I sit down for an initial consultation part of what I do is tell them that we will be communicating a lot. I ask them for what is the best number to contact them on. For most people this is their cell phone. I will call them right there, as their cell phone is ringing I will tell them that is me that is calling. I then say "Lets save each other's numbers now instead of trying to scroll through the call log". Just about one hundred percent of the time my contact info gets saved in their phones. I also will always keep their numbers in my phone. You will be pleasantly amazed at how warm and receptive your client or customer will be when you answer the phone "Hello Jim" instead of just "Hello" or your company name. Think about it, when you call your friend how do they answer the phone? That is how you should answer your phone.

When to Ask?

So often I think that most people ask for the referral or introduction at the wrong time. I hear so many trainings that state ask early, ask now, ask often. I have even heard people say ask as you are heading in the door, and ask as you are heading out the door.

Think for a moment how your customer or clients feel about what is your job description. Is it to solve a particular problem, put in the paperwork for a particular insurance plan, show me a particular house, and do my loan paperwork? Think for a moment what your customers feel what is your basic job. Now think about when all a real estate agent has done was show you some houses and then says "Who else can you refer me to that needs to by a house" (horrible language by the way). The customer or client may be thinking, you are doing your job nothing special. Let's look at this in a different light. How often in your industry can something happen that can cause major problems in your customer or client getting what they want? I am pretty sure that it happens on a regular basis. As the professionals that we are we typically figure out the solution and solve the problem. Once the problem is solved we typically never thing about it again. This is the perfect time to ask to be introduced to their friends, family, and coworkers! In order to earn the right to ask for an introduction there are some key steps that have to be followed.

First, blow the problem completely out of proportion. This problem can be the cause or reason your client or customer does not get their loan, house, car, or insurance. Keep in mind that your client or customer may panic at this point. And they are going to be looking to you for guidance to solve the problem. At this point if you do not have any recommendations for solutions, then you have put your customer or client in a panic tail spin.

Reassure the client or customer that you have a solution. Chat with them about possible solutions and give good quality recommendations on what should be their next best step. You have to do this during the same conversation. The last thing you want to do is to panic your customer or client and then have to research solutions forcing you to get back to them. Do your homework ahead of time! Sometimes the solution is something that does not need their input on. In this I still do this technique. It could be something as "Mr. Buyer the home that you want to purchase has a failed septic system. Because of this the home is not financeable and can be potentially condemned by the county health department. Remember when we first sat down and I told you about major problems, well this is one of the top problem makers out there." If you were mv buyer how are you feeling right about now? Normally after the shock has settled I continue "Now I know how important this home is to you and your family, and I know how important it is for you to be moved in before school starts. I have already started working with the agent that represents the seller, we have a licensed bonded septic company on site right this minute getting the septic system repaired. The silver lining in this cloud is that the septic system will be up to date, and warranted for parts and workmanship, I just wanted to keep you in the loop on what is going on." Now as my client, how do you feel about having me on your side?

At this point I am looking for the client to acknowledge what I just did for them. I want them to be appreciative of the fact that I did what was considered by them to be above and bcyond my job. Once I know that they are appreciative of what I just accomplished for them, I know at that point I have just earned the right to ask for an introduction (or referral) to their friends, family, or coworkers. And it is because they are so appreciative of what I just did for them, most of the time they are glad to introduce me to the people they know.

This chapter I would recommend reading at least three times. Your current clients and customers introducing you to their friends, family, and coworkers will be your best source of business. These will be people that will trust you and want to do business with you. Your cost of customer acquisition will be the lowest on attracting this business, along with the money that you will earn traditionally means that the business that is referred to you will become your highest rate of return. I have no problems running marketing campaigns that will generate new customers or clients, but I am always looking for ways to stay connected with my existing customers and clients to help make sure that I am in a position for them to recommend me to their friends, families, and coworkers.

Follow Up, Follow Up, Follow Up ... And if you missed it – Follow Up

Often people are surprised when I talk about the value of constant follow up while the sales is "in process". Most people in the sales world consider that once the deal is inked that the support staff is responsible for delivery of product and they should be onto the next prospect, customer, or client. Amazingly this is where most people start to lose the trust of their Realtor, Insurance Person, Financial Person, and so forth. Keeping in contact with your customer or client through the sales process is crucial in becoming known as the "Friend in the Business"

Think for a moment what your competition does. They meet with a prospect, do a needs and wants analyses, shows options, overcomes objections if needed, negotiate, and close the sale. If you look at most sales books, trainers, and techniques this is pretty much a blue print plan in most trainings. Imagine for a moment what the customer of client experiences.

First they experience the meeting of someone that hopefully will take care of them. It does not matter what your product or service is for the most part the consumer could get what they need without dealing with what they view as a "salesperson". The reason that they normally will sit down and subject themselves to meeting with a "salesperson" is because they want someone that will help them make the best decision. Even for most of the people that I work with that require a license to sell the product or service that they do, most of the time if the consumer wanted to they could bypass the "salesperson".

Next the consumer goes through some ones presentation, they may or may not bring up concerns (we call these objections) and makes a decision to move forward with your product or service. The consumer is happy in the moment because they have accomplished something that they either needed or wanted to get done. At a certain point they customer or client may start to question their decision. This is what we call buyer's remorse, the consumer calls this "did I make the right choice?"

Now if you are doing what the majority of sales professional people are doing, you may have already moved onto the next prospect, client, or customer. Anyone that has ever been in a pure one hundred percent commission position knows that in order to keep your income moving in the right direction that it is needed to be moving on to the next available prospect, client, or customer. I want you to think for a moment what your client or customer is going through. When the salesperson no longer communicates directly to their client of customer before the sale is complete. This is when the customer or client feels that the salesperson was just a salesperson and not a trusted advisor, or a friend that was there to take care of them. This is where most people in the sales industry fail at becoming known as the "Friend in the Business".

I can hear you know, but Greg if I spend all my time following up with the customer before delivery I will never be able to meet with my next customer and my months will look like a yo-yo. One month eating steak, the next month crackers. Trust me I know how you feel, you may or may not know is that I am also a Realtor. So these techniques are not just something I think works great, they have also been personally tested by myself.

As we talked about the average Realtor, Insurance person, Financial rep, or fill in your industry once the deal has been inked they are off to the next meeting. I can understand that as a successful person in these industries that part of our job is getting prospects through the sales funnel and moving them into happy loyal customers or clients. I am going to challenge you to see how you can add time into your week to touch base with client's or customers when they have gone from agreeing to the sale (or inking the contract) to receiving the product or service that they have bought.

When I personally discovered the importance of this technique was when I sat down and figured out how much time I would spend on the phone if my client had initiated the call to me for an update. I then looked at how much time I spent on the call when I initiated the call to update the client on the progress of the inspection, financing, or closing of escrow. Now in the times that I only had one client, it was easy to let them call me, heck normally I had nothing else to do but talk to them. As anyone in this situation knows when this is the case I was eating steak the day after closing, crackers the next month. As I learned and perfected how to become known as "The Friend in the Real Estate Business" I quickly saw my client list grow. For me out of necessity I had to set aside two to three hours a week to do in process follow up calls. Ironically after I started doing the follow up calls my referrals went up and I had more time to work with new clients.

Think for a moment about your product or service. What is your sales cycle in how long it takes to go from "closing the sale" to delivery of the product or service. The armature wants to think that once they have the client or customer sign the bottom line that their job is done. If this is the case then that person will also experience having to constantly go out and look for fresh prospects. The professional that understands the importance of taking care of their clients or customer, along with staying in touch with them in what most of the time they think that your job is over with will show them how much you do care about them and do not see them as just a "commission check". In following up with your clients or customers during the sales process will help develop a friendship, along with open conversations for referral opportunities, and help establish you as their "Friend in the Business"

Staying Connected After the Sale

For the majority of people in sales industry they view that once the sale has been made and the product has been delivered to the customer or client most people in sales drop off the face of the earth. Maybe the sales person will connect every once in a while when they have nothing better to do, and not sure how to handle the accord moment of what to do and not look like a pushy sales person. I am reminded by this from a client of mine that told me that I did a great job of staying in touch with her during the transaction, was always there for her and her family during the whole process. Then after they received the keys they never heard from me again. It was in this experience that I realized that I was not just their real estate broker, that I had not realized I also became a friend. At least until I messed it up by not staying connected. Needless to say, I have not made that mistake since.

So how to stay connected and in touch with your client or customers. I consider it to be a double bladed sword that we now have technology to help us and assist us on staying connected with our clients and customers. The other side of the sword is that while technology helps us to stay connected, if our follow up is dripping of that of technology and automation, we have lost the effect of the staying connected and have turned our client or customer into feeling that of a paycheck and not a friend.

One of the best practices of staying connected to someone is the value of using personal notes. Now I know of at least one service that will write your personal note, and even put a real stamp on it (not a machine, but the same type of stamp you can purchase at the post office). I tried this service out briefly, the response I got was something to the effect of thank you for the card, why was it postmarked out of Salt Lake City? The reason for this question was the fact that at the time I lived just south of Seattle Washington. Even with the "handwritten" font, it was painfully obesely that this system was automated and not truly a handwritten personal note.

Another note on the hand written note make it relevant and about your customer or client. I have heard of other trainers push that to send five hand written notes a day. I started seeing people sending notes of "was just thinking about you ... and I am always hear for your referrals". I looked at those notes almost being desperate and boarding on being a stalker. My recommendation is that when you see a customer or client or see something that is relevant to them, then send them a quick note. I have seeing just sending a note of thanks will lead to a great amount of trust from your customer or client to you.

So when it comes to personal notes I would put a higher value on the quality of the notes you are able to write and send out as oppose to the quantity of notes that you send out. Remember that you always want to make the personal note about the customer or client, not about what you are doing. Some great examples of when to send out a note:

Seeing them out and about, ask to get together for coffee to catch up

To thank them for introducing you to a friend, family, or coworker

You noticed a mile stone for their career in the paper

Birthday Cards

Another aspect of staying connected with your clients or customers is in the form of mailers. Now something to keep in mind is that if the majority of your clients or customers are millennials, they tend to not to be to found of getting a lot of mail. If they happen to be older (baby boomer for example) they are used to getting mail. I would recommend that you gage this according to what your market would expect. When I first started mailing, I would purchase a newsletter to send to my clients. The bad thing about this newsletter was that it had nothing about me and more important nothing about the local real estate markets (what is what my clients most cared about). What I did was I backed off the mailing to quarterly (as this was enough for both my millennials and baby boomer clients) and it was a letter written by me. What I did was I would include a personal event in my life giving humor. I would put a paragraph on a recent person that I helped (this would help give ideals of who they could introduce me to) and I would end it with some item of value of what was happening in the local real estate market. When I started using this approach on my mailings I personally saw a huge increase in my clients reaching out to me.

Another way to stay connected is to touch base with your customers on the phone. Make time to reach out to them and to just connect. This technique, just like the mailings will have to be personally tailored to your client or customer. If they are a phone talking person, then great. If not then it may be best to send them a quick text. So often I will set up a time to call people about every three to four months. Traditionally I say that I just wanted to catch up with them and felt that it has been to long since we last chatted. I never go into these calls looking for business. Several times it will lead to an introduction or two.

The new world of social media has also allowed us to help stay connected to our clients or customers. There are several social media platforms out there. My recommendation on the use of social media in staying connected is to pick the top platforms that you see best connecting to your clients or customers. Once you have identified those platforms, learn them and use them to stay connected. After that look at and see what platforms you can use to help market and promote your product or service. Remember that social media is constantly changing and you must stay up to date on how to use social media. Don't be afraid to use a new platform, if it doesn't take for your industry then drop it.

The majority of your competition will either rarely or never do anything to stay connected with their clients or customers after the sale has been made. This is on one hand very sad as the customer probably put a great deal of trust in the person (especially in the real estate, insurance, or financial services industry) and will feel let down when they never hear from their trusted advisor. The good side about this is that those of us that put a priority on making our clients and customers into our friends will find people that will always think of us when they hear about someone that can use our product or service.

Staying Connected by Providing Value

What product or service do you provide for your client or customer? As a real estate broker the service that I provide for my clients is that of helping them buy and sell real estate. Now if all I focused on for providing value was when they had a real estate question or concern, well I would only hear from my clients once every five to seven year. Expecting them to remember me after five to seven years may be asking a lot.

They're several ways to stay connected with your customers and clients and we will be covering those in the next chapter. In this chapter I want us to focus on how to stay top of mind awareness with your customers and clients. This step will truly help you progress from "the person that helped us buy (fill in the blank)" to "My friend that helps people get (fill in the blank)". This is the one step that I see most people fail on than any other, and by mastering this step it will help you generate more referrals than doing cold marketing will.

I have discovered that I want to become a resource for my customers and clients. I want them to think about me whenever they have a question or concern. Now on the down side this means that I do take a lot of calls and help connect people with services that have nothing to do with my business of real estate. On the plus side of this whenever my clients have a concern, I am one of the first people that they reach out to.

This means that I am able to stay top of mind with them.

How do you become a resource? This will take some work on your side. First step is to get active within your business community. This can be done either as a Chamber of Commerce member, a member of a leads group, or becoming very active with networking groups. Look at products or services that your customer or clients would need and would like a trusted reputable person or business to get them from. Start networking and build relationships with these business or service providers.

In my "resource directory" I have everything in there from the obvious contractors, plumbers, movers and such. I also have what I call the not so obvious. This list includes computer people, an automobile repair facility, a jeweler, a D.J., and several others that are not involved in the real estate industry.

I learned this technique from a great friend of mine that is a real estate coach and trainer. What this does is it helps me to network with other people that can refer business to me. This also allows me to refer business to those people that I do business with and know that they will take great care of my customers or clients. When let's take for example Scott who is my automobile repair guy has one of my friends walk in, Scott becomes appreciative of my recommendation. My hope is that when Scott has a real estate need, or one of his employees or friends or family members has a real estate need that Scott remembers me.

Now Scott does not provide me a kick back, or a commission, or any type of "finder's fee" for my recommendation. I would highly recommend that you do NOT allow yourself to take any type of compensation for your referrals. I have been offered by people (not Scott by the way) a referral fee. I have always politely declined it and ask that they apply it as a credit to my client's bill. I do this for a few reasons, the biggest reason is that I do not want my recommendations to be influenced by direct financial compensation. When I hand over my "resource directory" to my clients I tell them that nobody in this book has paid to be in the book, nobody in this book has helped contribute to the cost of putting together the book. What this also helps is in the situation where I feel that someone that was in the book, no longer has the same morals or values as I do, it becomes very easy to remove them from the book. I really want you to understand the importance of finding great service providers that will take care of your customers and clients in the same way that you take care of them. If I recommend a person for one of my clients and they do not take care of them, their poor service can have a negative impact on me also.

By having these people and companies in my resource directory it allows me to connect with each of them. I try to at least once a year, and prefer to connect on a quarterly basis. When I find out one of my clients has utilized the product or service from someone in my resource directory I also follow up. What this does is it helps me to stay top of mind of those in my resource directory too. About once a year I do also look at is the relationship beneficial for both myself and the person that is in my resource directory. And is the relationship also beneficial to my clients. For my contacts in my resource directory this is the only form of compensation that I do look at. I do take into consideration of if they are also helping me get referrals from their network, or if they are just enjoying receiving referrals from myself or my network.

I will warn you that this step can be one of the longer steps on how to become known as the Friend in The Business. When I decided to put together my resource directory it took almost nine months from thought to actually having it. Part of this was to make sure of who I wanted to put into the book, surveying my clients to discover who they most needed, along with determining how to put my book together (mine ultimately became a business card holder with my contact info imprinted on the front). Once it is put together it will become very easy to maintain. For me when we help someone either purchase or sell a piece of real estate, this is an item that we give to them. It also sets up the stage that if they have any needs that they can always call me for a great recommendation. Think for a moments, when was the last time you called your real estate broker for a recommendation for a place to have work done on your car, when was the last time you asked a friend for the same recommendation?

Now Go Forth and Become The Friend in the Business!

As you can see becoming known as the friend in the business is a great thing to do. Becoming known as the friend in the business typically does not happen by accident. Becoming the friend in the business does take some work and does take some effort, and I can tell you from my own personal experience that becoming the friend in the business is a rewarding feeling.

Just like anything else I would recommend that you start on one item that you feel will add the most value to your own personal business. Invest in that one item and start putting into place the first part of that item. So many people I see fail as they try to do everything at once and then become overwhelmed. As you have read in this book look for the one thing you want to put into place and then spend the next couple of weeks putting it into play. After that pick the next item and start putting that into place. If it takes you six months or more to put everything in this book into place that is ok.

I see so many people that will boast that they have been in business for ten or more years. And when I look at their business model I realize that they have one year of business that they have redone for ten plus years. This is a scary business model as it is dependent on the person to not only be a great practitioner of what they do, it also requires that they are constantly marketing and advertising to get the next batch of leads to work. By designing your business model for that of becoming known as the "Friend in the Business" you actually help create a sales force of people out their marketing and promoting you! So you are not recreating your first year ten plus times, you are actually building a stronger business each and every year!

I look forward to hearing from you on how you have become the friend in the business! I would love to hear and you can always email me at GregTSpeaker@Gmail.com